T · H · E
DUTIFUL PENGUIN

BY THE SAME AUTHOR

Light and Shadow, Fourteen Sonnets
published by Bright Angel Publishing Company, 1982.

T · H · E
DUTIFUL PENGUIN

ZOOLOGY IN VERSE

BY
RICHARD BUCKLEY

Bright Angel
Publishing
Company

THE DUTIFUL PENGUIN
ZOOLOGY IN VERSE
BY RICHARD BUCKLEY

BRIGHT ANGEL PUBLISHING COMPANY · CHELTENHAM

First published in 1985 in Great Britain by Bright Angel Publishing Company,
One Lansdown Parade, Cheltenham, Gloucestershire GL50 2LH.

Designed by Tony Price Studios, 6 Imperial Square, Cheltenham.
Typesetting by Promenade Photosetting Limited, 6 Imperial Square, Cheltenham.
Printed by Cotswold Printing Company Limited, Stroud.

Text set in Meridien Roman

British Library Cataloguing in Publication Data

Buckley, Richard
The dutiful penguin: zoology in verse.
I. Title
821′.914 PR6052.U9

ISBN 0-947921-00-1

TO MY SONS
SEBASTIAN AND BENEDICT

ACKNOWLEDGEMENTS

The illustrations in this book are based on Victorian designs and engravings by the Brothers Dalziel, W.S. Coleman, Zwecker and other artists unknown.

We gratefully acknowledge the following sources:

Art for Commerce,
published by The Scolar Press in 1973.

Early Advertising Art,
published by Dover Publications Inc. in 1953.

Illustrated Natural History by the Rev. J.G. Wood,
published by George Routledge and Sons in 1869.

The Pictorial Museum of Animated Nature,
published by Charles Knight & Co. in 1856-58.

A Source Book of French Advertising Art,
published by Faber and Faber in 1964.

CONTENTS

8
The Dutiful Penguin

10
The Imprudent Kangaroo

12
The Platypus

14
The Schizophrenic Hippopotamus

16
The Ant

18
The Beautiful Camel

20
The Mole

22
The Whale

24
The Dissatisfied Elephant

26
The Ostrich

28
Metamorphosis

29
The Crocodile

30
The Universal Dog

32
The Greedy Python

33
The Amoeba

34
The Lazy Lion

36
The Dolphin

38
The Description of a Horse

40
The Foolish Tortoise

THE DUTIFUL PENGUIN

Now the lives of the world's many creatures
  Are all wonderfully different you know,
And their conduct of childhood has features
  Which are stranger than fiction could show.

The koalas keep children in pouches,
  Have marsupial pockets of fun;
Baby storks live high up in the branches,
  Get as close as they can to the sun.

Some beasts bury their children to hide them,
  That's why turtles lay eggs in the sand,
But the penguins, though I don't deride them,
  They have habits I can't understand.

The South Pole is where they do their mating,
  And the hatching is done in deep freeze
And the male stands all winter just waiting,
  With an egg on his foot, if you please!

Penguin fathers are genuine heroes,
  They don't flinch when the icicles form
And in temperatures well below zero
  Somehow manage to keep the eggs warm.

Day and night on the ice over Yule-tide,
  Braving blizzards and winds like a whip,
While their wives are away at the seaside,
  Eating well and enjoying the trip,

All the menfolk stand huddled together
   And they shiver from ankle to nose,
Until spring brings a break in the weather
   And the sun melts the ice on their toes.

Now the penguin may not be a beauty,
   When he walks he's a figure of fun,
But the penguin's devotion to duty –
   That must surely be second to none.

THE IMPRUDENT KANGAROO

Kangaroos, as you probably know,
Are born while they're still embryo,
It takes eight months at least
    Before these strange beasts
Can their mothers' protection forego.

But there once was a child kangaroo
Who displayed such great derring-do
That he started to climb
    Before the right time
From the pouch where he'd lived hitherto.

This precocious and bold quadruped,
Though still he was only half-bred,
From his safe normal place
    Leapt out into space
And crashed down rather hard on his head.

But in spite of this unpleasant fall,
The young fool learned nothing at all;
Cursing fortune unjust,
    He brushed off the dust,
Then he jumped through a gap in a wall.

To the outback headed this stranger,
This small inexpert bushranger,
Where he started to bound
    All over the ground
With reckless contempt for the danger.

He fell in a hole with his first leap,
Disturbing wombats from their sleep.
With his next spring I've heard,
    This joey absurd
Got impaled on a white cockatoo's beak.

As he then steeplechased up a tree,
The koalas turned round to flee
And an emu close by
    Attempted to fly,
A laughing jackass screeched with glee.

Soon after, this bouncing beginner,
Still rash but now looking thinner,
Hopped along the wrong track
    Fell down on his back
And a dingo had him for dinner.

The kangaroo mob started weeping;
The boomer, roused from his sleeping,
Said: "The lesson is plain,
    I'll say it again.
Always look before you go leaping."

THE PLATYPUS

I don't wish to offend
But I don't comprehend
That creature down there in the sand.
It's got fur like a bear
  But webbed feet I declare
Are made for the water, not land.

It's most oddly designed;
Though a beaver behind,
It's more like a duck at the front.
It lays eggs like a bird,
  Such behaviour's absurd,
Like some sort of Hollywood stunt.

It's no teeth in its jaws,
Has four claws not four paws
And has milk but no sign of teats;
It swims fast as a shark
  But it swims in the dark,
Its physique all logic defeats.

Did Darwin invent it?
A do-it-yourself kit
With pieces mixed up in the box?
Was it done to provoke?
    Like a practical joke,
Poking fun at life's paradox?

Was it made by machines?
Or explosion of genes?
Was it folly, freak or a fake?
Was it Friday-produced?
    From a UFO unloosed?
Or did God just make a mistake?

THE SCHIZOPHRENIC HIPPOPOTAMUS

The hippo, in his peaceful way,
Prefers to wallow through the day
And sleep to pass the time away
  With other hippos in a pool,
  Not just to keep his body cool,
  But following a social rule
Which strictly bids our handsome friend
To gather closely end to end
And makes each yawning hippo spend
  His pachydermal afternoon
  Where he can snore or swim or spoon
  In languid river or lagoon.

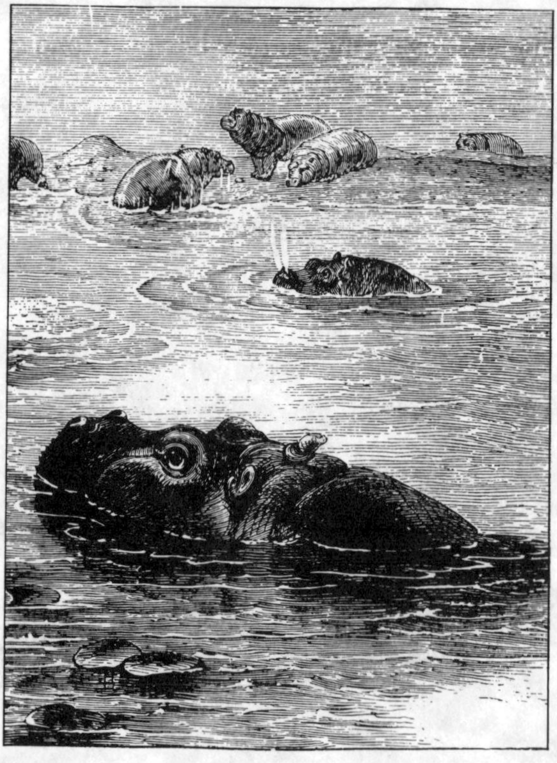

At night, however, I've been told
Hippo demeanour's less controlled,
Instead of being good as gold,
  He goes berserk, mad raving stark,
  Runs riot in his wildlife park,
  Creating mayhem in the dark,
Careering through the undergrowth,
Behaving like some drunken oaf,
Completely off his hippo loaf,
  Befouling tail and jungle trail,
  Attacking every passing male,
  And making even lions quail.

But why should such a gentle beast
  Become a raving loon
As soon as daylight hours have ceased
  And sun's replaced by moon?
It's one of nature's mysteries,
  Still unexplained by man;
But learn from such hippo-crisy
  This lesson if you can:
When character you wish to judge,
  Appearances the truth may fudge.
That Doctor Jekyll you've described
  Could also be a Mister Hyde.

THE ANT

O'er ground a rapid ambulant,
With legs a strong appurtenant,
Abdomen shining luminant,
Antennae as communicant
And jaws a bit protuberant,
The ant, the tiny ant.

The queen's a pregnant emigrant,
The male goes as concomitant
And on the wing both procreant
To start a new nest germinant,
O'er eggs and larvae vigilant,
The ant, the parent ant.

Of earth and woods the habitant,
Of complex tunnels fabricant,
Of aphids the agricolant,
Of discipline the postulant,
Of holidays quite ignorant,
The ant, the busy ant.

In sharing he's unhesitant,
With fellow ants collaborant,
Not arrogant, not petulant,
He's generous to the mendicant
But punishes the miscreant,
The ant, the social ant.

Of friends the trusty confidant,
Of enemies brave combatant,
In sacrifice extravagant,
In bearing loads he's nonchalant,
When duty calls he's adamant,
The ant, the noble ant.

Untrousered and yet elegant,
In human pants an irritant,
His sting's a painful penetrant,
Though smaller than an elephant
The ant's not insignificant,
The ant, the tiny ant.

THE BEAUTIFUL CAMEL

Down in the Sahara
    Bathtime's very quick,
Water is too precious
    For more than just a lick.

Down among the sand dunes
    In the desert's glare,
Washing for the camel's
    A very brief affair.

All day without water,
    Sometimes all the week,
Plodding through the dustbowl
    Parading in the heat.

Friend of every bedouin,
    Source of wealth and pride,
Since without the camel
    No nomad rider rides.

Onward to the skyline
    Beast with burden goes,
Bearing bags and baggage,
    Hot hump and blistered toes.

Then a green oasis
    Shimmers in the sun.
Is it just a mirage?
    The camel starts to run.

Kneels down by the water,
    Pours it down his throat,
Gallon after gallon,
    You'd think his hump would float.

Camels smell quite dreadful,
   Suffer from bad breath.
Camels have foul tempers,
   Their bite can lead to death.

Camels look peculiar,
   Lumpy on their backs,
Camel stomachs hang down
   Like half-full haversacks.

Looks are unimportant
   When your life is tough.
Down in the Sahara,
   Just to survive's enough.

So admire the camel,
   Follow in his tracks.
Water and not beauty
   Is what the desert lacks.

THE MOLE

The mole's secret life,
  Like that of his wife,
Is invisible,
  Even risible.
His habitat droll's
  In dirty damp holes;
He shares worms' eye view –
  And eats the worms too.

This insectivore,
  Whose talent's to bore,
Who burrows unseen
  Down under the green,
This earth troglodyte
  Lives out of the light –
The mole doesn't mind,
  He's more or less blind.

He scorns the fresh air,
  The sun's dazzling glare,
His preference is dark
  And Hyde not Green Park.
He tunnels for food
  When he's in the mood –
That's both day and night
  With his appetite.

A black velvet coat
    This talpid denotes;
With five spadelike claws
    On bulldozer paws,
Fossorial feet
    To excavate deep
Below in the loam
    An underground home.

He's not mining coal
    Or chasing a vole
Or digging for gold
    Or fleeing the cold
Or burying bones
    Or looking for stones
Or drilling for oil
    Down there in the soil.

I'm sure that the role,
    The goal of the mole
Is staying at large
    To do sabotage
With ridges and mounds
    And holes in the ground –
While I sleep till dawn,
    He ruins the lawn.

THE WHALE

You say that the whale is a mammal?
With vestigial limbs front and back?
It's just like a dog or a camel?
Or a horse or a cow or a cat?

In my view, the whale's an impostor,
It's a fish, not a mammal at all,
A fraud that you scientists foster,
I'm quite taken aback at your gall.

Can mammals live out in the ocean?
Spend their days in the watery deep?
I must say that seems an odd notion,
Do they lie on the seabed to sleep?

Would mammals support all that blubber?
Would they float through the waves without care?
A mammal is such a land lubber,
It would certainly get mal de mer.

A mammal's supposed to have four legs
And some fur or at least a few hairs.
A whale's just as smooth as a goose egg,
It's a trait which in mammals is rare.

You say whales give birth underwater?
Well, that proves whales are fish pseudonyms.
How else could they teach sons and daughters
To come straight from the womb and then swim?

A mammal prefers to breathe fresh air,
That's quite difficult under the sea.
Can whale blowholes with noses compare?
That's the next thing you'll try telling me!

But why waste our time on this question
Whether whales to the mammals are linked,
Let's deal with another suggestion,
That the whales may quite soon be extinct.

THE DISSATISFIED ELEPHANT

"To have ears such as mine is not at all nice,"
Said the elephant baby more than just twice,
"They're too big and besides they get in a flap
Each time that the wind blows too hard from the back."

"And there's more than one blemish I must endure,"
Said this miserable jumbo in miniature,
"My skin is so rough that I feel quite shamefaced,
Why even the snakes look at me with distaste."

"My nose is so long that it hangs to my knees
And the leaves on the trees fall down when I sneeze.
My tusks are immense and they get in the way
When I clean my back teeth at close of the day."

"My feet are too big for the largest of shoes,
My tail is too short to do more than amuse,
I wish, how I wish that I could just have been
One of the other beasts that I've sometimes seen."

Said his much much older and wiser papa,
"Be thankful from others you're dissimilar,
We heavyweight mammals have luck on our side,
You've no reason to feel so dissatisfied."

"Your skin was made thick to protect you from pain,
Your ears give you hearing (and shelter from rain!),
Your tusks will defend you from rivals malign,
Your tail's a fine flywhisk attached to your spine."

"Your foot, in proportion to your body size,
Can your torso support and then mobilise,
Your trunk is an organ that's both hand and nose,
Without it, dear fellow, you'd be indisposed."

"Be thankful, young fool, for the gifts God bestowed,
It's better to travel along your own road;
What's not yours don't envy, don't live in reproach,
You might have been born as a baby cockroach."

THE OSTRICH

The ostrich is a funny bird
Two yards or more in height,
Three hundred pounds on two-toed feet
With twenty/twenty sight.

The ostrich is ridiculous,
His neck's a metre long,
He swallows stones and sand and bones
To help his meals along.

The ostrich is a comic bird,
Has eggs laid by the ton
With shells so tough they're strong enough
For men to walk upon.

The ostrich is incongruous,
Because he's desert bred,
His feathers are not waterproof
And damp gets in his head.

The ostrich is a rum old bird,
He likes to dominate,
But in retreat his self-conceit
Is inappropriate.

The ostrich is fatuitous,
When danger is around,
He hits the deck and holds his neck
Stretched out across the ground.

The ostrich is a clumsy bird,
An aeronautic clown,
With heavy bones and stubby wings,
He can't get off the ground.

The ostrich is preposterous,
  His voice does not belong,
Sounds serpentine or leonine
  And not a bit like song.

The ostrich is a curious bird
  Whose feathers make fine hats,
Or fancy fans for French cancans,
  Or plumes for diplomats.

The ostrich is hilarious,
  With legs just like a horse,
He's just as fast and yet alas
  He cannot stay the course.

The ostrich is a funny bird,
  The butt of human wit.
But if your head's deep in the sand
  Can you still laugh at it?

Metamorphosis

Starting life in a water-bound bubble,
Packed up tight in a sac on my back,
Always hoping to float clear of trouble
When, out looking for gudgeon or bream,
Nature lovers hang hooks in the stream.

This new tail's like some eely hindquarters
And the comma ending this line,
Down I dive and drive round in the water,
Plunge about like a boat with no steering
Or dart like a sprat through the brine.
Later on, though my tail's disappearing,
Extra long jointed legs will be mine.

For the last part I'm fully amphibian,
Roaming either by water or earth,
Outmanoeuvring fish or pedestrian,
Got twin life from my strange triple birth.

THE CROCODILE

Oh crocodile,
Despite your smile,
You're not a friendly chap.
Behind that grin
The teeth begin
And form a deadly trap.

Just at the thought
Of being caught
I fall into a faint.
I'd run a mile
From crocodile
However queer or quaint.

Oh crocodile,
I fear your guile,
False tears conceal your glee;
That log afloat
Beside my boat
Has yellow eyes on me.

Oh crocodile,
Oh dark reptile,
Though I won't swim near you,
That doesn't mean
I wish you'd been
A handbag or a shoe.

THE UNIVERSAL DOG

When a Samoyed and greyhound
Meet a mastiff and a bloodhound
And a dachshund and a Maltese,
Each canine crony wags his tail.

If a poodle and a pointer
Take a schnauzer and a pinscher
Along to see a Pekingese,
The conversation never fails.

When a spaniel and a bulldog
Go to dinner with a sheepdog,
They might sit next to a collie
Or meet some Weimaraner friends.

You may see an Irish setter
With both Airedale and Skye terrier
Taking tea with a Welsh corgi
And sniffing at each other's ends.

When it comes to saying bow wow
A chihuahua and a chow chow
And a beagle and a basset
Can understand each other's bark.

For the boxer and the Great Dane,
The puli, pug and Pomerane,
The retriever and the whippet
All sailed as wolves in Noah's ark.

Which explains why the Alsatians
Are similar to Dalmatians,
Like the borzoi and saluki,
They tend to stop at every tree.

Of different colour, shape and size,
Dogs come in multifarious guise,
Yet mongrel or a pedigree,
They share a common ancestry.

In some respects, as you can see,
A dog is just like you and me.

THE GREEDY PYTHON

Peter the Python would frequently boast
He'd eat anything – raw, boiled, steamed or roast.
He'd start with a rat or maybe a frog,
Go on with a bat and end with a dog.
He'd hang from a branch and watch beasts beneath,
Then gobble them up with back-pointing teeth,
His tail coiled around to squeeze them quite flat
Whatever their shape – tall, short, thin or fat.
He'd open his jaws and swallow his prey,
Then slowly digest the rest of the day.

No-one was exempt from his appetite,
A fish in the pond was gone in one bite,
A bird in the bush would soon disappear,
A jackal, a goat, a duiker, a deer
Once in his clutches had no breathing space,
Rabbits in hutches weren't in a safe place,
A porcupine too might meet the same fate,
Resulting in piles of quills on Pete's plate.

For gluttonous feats the snake was renowned,
But greed though he had his mind was unsound,
For one fateful day when hunger had struck,
He bit off too much and ran out of luck.
He saw his own tail then ruined his health,
With one mighty gulp, he swallowed himself.

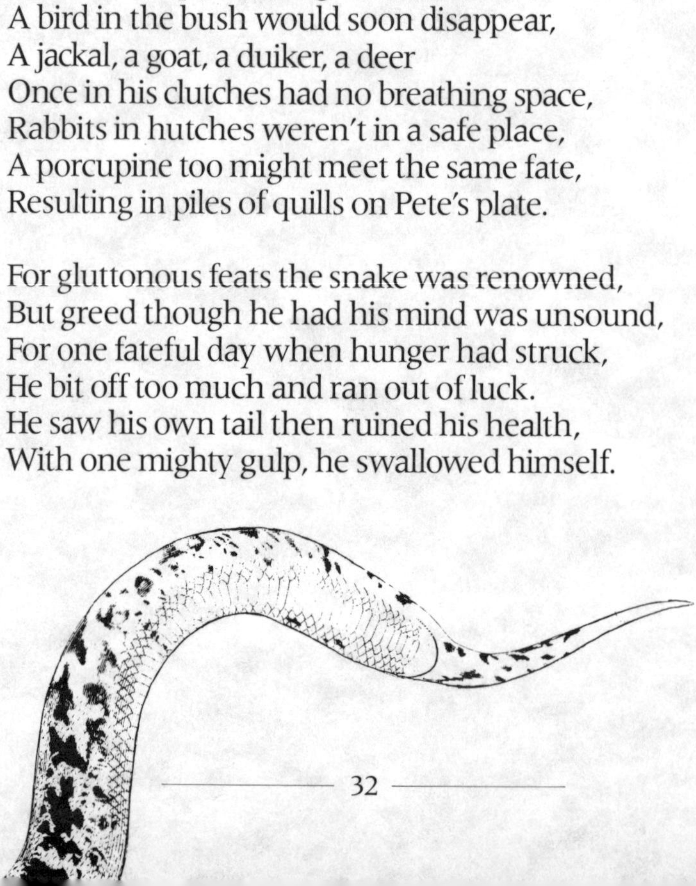

THE AMOEBA

The amoeba's so small
That it strains human eyes
Except on a microscope slide,
But it knows how to crawl
Pseudopodia-wise
And knows which direction to glide.

It is able to eat
Without stomach or mouth
By protoplasmic ingestion,
It can even excrete
From its north or its south
Which helps to stop indigestion.

It does not feel the cold,
Suffer pain or show rage,
It knows neither poorness nor wealth.
It can never get old,
When it nears middle age,
It simply replaces itself.

Its own reproduction
Involves no seduction,
It needs neither husband nor wife.
  All this prompts one to say
    That amoebae display
        Some signs of intelligent life.

THE LAZY LION

Old Leo is the jungle king,
  A savage tawny slinker;
But not so much an active king,
  He's more a forty winker.

Yes Leo is a lazy beast,
  Who likes things soporific,
And even though he likes to feast,
  His hunting's unterrific.

The lion ladies game must chase
  While he just lies in waiting,
For exercise is not his taste
  (Unless it's time for mating).

He stays in bed till noon at least,
  Snores loudly without stopping,
Yes Leo is a lazy beast,
  His forte is off-dropping.

And so he sleeps, this jungle lord,
  Surrounded by his spouses,
Till gradually they all get bored
  And fidget while he drowses.

Then one day comes another male,
A handsome curly maner,
Who winks his eye and wags his tail –
His aims could not be plainer.

While lord and master stays shut-eyed,
Each wife turns restless rover,
And soon poor Leo's lost his pride,
His rival's taken over.

The lazy lion's great mistake
Serves as a timely warning –
A jungle king must stay awake,
Not sleep throughout the morning.

THE DOLPHIN

They say the dolphin's friendly,
Seeks the company of man,
Carries people on his back
Like a good Samaritan.

They say the dolphin's loyal
And will stick through thick and thin,
In seaweed, storm or oil,
He will never lose his grin.

They say the dolphin's talking
When he whistles to his mates,
It's not just pointless squawking,
It's how he communicates.

In ultrasonic noises
With his fellows he'll discuss,
Thus bottlenoses' voices
Are inaudible to us.

As for the dolphin's swimming,
It's the wonder of the world,
Across the wavetops skimming
Like a cork that's just been hurled.

Occasionally leaping
Thirty feet into the air,
Such joyfulness in keeping
With a dolphin's debonair,

This submarine cavorter
Rides white horses with his friends,
Or dives into the water
Without suffering the bends.

This dolphin who's so cheering,
Who is harmless as a fish,
Whose habits are endearing,
Who is man's antithesis,

Who's happy in his virtue,
Who's intelligent and true –
It really can't surprise you
That we put him in a zoo.

THE DESCRIPTION OF A HORSE

To give a horse description is far from an easy task,
It's not a simple matter of a beast that feeds on grass.
Arabian or mustang, Shetland pony or a shire,
The rules for equine profiles provide something to admire.

Is this horse wearing stockings? and does that present a blaze?
Is it one of the sorrels? or is it one of the bays?
Is it an appaloosa? or a piebald, dun or roan?
Is it a palomino? or some other type unknown?

It might be colt or filly, gelding, stallion or mare,
Perhaps a saddle palfrey or one of a coach and pair.
How many hands are measured from the withers to the ground?
And do its teeth look healthy? are its legs and muscles sound?

Do any feet have shoeboils? are its leg joints thoroughpinned?
Are there the signs of sand-crack? has it worms or broken wind?
Or are its ears up-pointing and its habits disciplined?
Its eyes both clear and sparkling, both its mane and tail well trimme

And what about the gaskins, cannons, fetlocks and the shanks?
Not mentioning the chestnuts, pasterns, coronets and flanks,
The forearms and the elbows, buttocks, back and point of hip,
The muzzle and the chin groove, forelock, crest and underlip,

The barrel, girth and shoulder, and the neck, the loin, the hock,
Croup, cheek and chest and stifle, the poll, abdomen and dock?
The connoisseurs of horses will examine every part,
Their quadrupedic survey is a scientific art.

The words they use get stranger, would an amateur dismay,
But do not scorn these symbols which all equine shapes portray;
The lexicon of horseflesh is much more than just a game,
If "nag" is all we called him, would a horse still look the same?

THE FOOLISH TORTOISE

When he's competing in a race,
A tortoise doesn't have the pace
To show a hare his rear.
He's no good in a steeplechase
Nor can he drive his carapace
Except in bottom gear.

This simple fact is very plain,
You'll really have to look again
If speed is what you seek,
For turtles' talents aren't the same
As rabbits' or impala game's –
They haven't the physique.

Yet once a tortoise (so I'm told),
When he was barely three years old,
Did long for greater dash
And to that end his shell he sold,
An act which made him feel the cold
And some thought rather rash.

Untroubled by his fellows' scorn,
Untrammelled by their heavy horn,
He skipped across the ground.
His absent shell he did not mourn,
The fastest tortoise ever born
The critics did confound.

This racing tortoise said farewell:
"At last I've shed that silly shell
And got it off my back!
In locomotion I'll excel,
Aerodynamically as well,
Once I have got the knack!"

The foolish creature packed his bag,
Continuing the while to brag
About his gait so brisk.
His anxious mother meanwhile nags:
"In going shell-less there are snags,
You should not take the risk."

"It's good for you your tortoise shell,
Provides a home where you can dwell,
(A mobile home at that),
And furthermore you can repel
All enemies with that hard shell
From crocodile to cat."

Her son his mirth could scarcely quell:
"My speed is now my citadel
To keep me safe from harm.
And as for home, your fears dispel,
I'll lodge myself in an hotel.
Please, mother, do keep calm."

With that the tortoise breakfast ate,
One last good meal upon his plate
Before he went away.
His mother said:
"This blanket take
In case you want to hibernate
Along the broad highway."

Of all the beasts on land or sea
Chelonian longevity
Has much the longest span,
It's frequently a century.
This traveller was barely three
When his new life began.

And he was three, as you may guess,
Exactly that, no more no less,
When lease of life expired.
Though faster, he was not express,
He could not reach the rapidness
To which he had aspired.

That night the young fool walking late,
With no defence testudinate,
A hungry fox did smell.
The tortoise fled, but much too late
And soon he cried disconsolate:
"I wish I'd kept my shell!"

THE END

ABOUT THE AUTHOR

Richard Buckley is a freelance writer and editor.
He is also a chartered accountant and, in addition to poetry, short stories and children's books, has written extensively on business and professional subjects.
He worked in New York for five years and has travelled in North and South America, Central Asia and Europe.
He now lives in Gloucestershire with his Austrian wife Elfie and their two sons Sebastian and Benedict.